Popular Patterns of

Flow Blue China

with Prices

Veneita Mason

All photographs by Robert J. Cook

Burlington, Iowa

Front Cover: Plates—Astoria. Cups and saucers—Clayton.

Butter pats—Jewel. Creamer—Oriental.

Large sugar—Chapoo. Small sugar—Argyle.

Relish dish or underplate—Marechal Niel. Jardiniere—English pattern.

In the corner cupboard: Touraine.

Library of Congress
Catalog Number 81-71156

ISBN 0-87069-400-6

10   9   8   7   6   5   4   3   2

Published by

Wallace-Homestead
authoritative books on antiques & collectibles

Wallace-Homestead Book Company
1912 Grand Avenue
Des Moines, Iowa 50305

To my husband Walter W. Mason

whose loving support helped make this

book a reality.

Contents

Foreword

My mother and grandmother had lovely blue and white dishes, which may explain why I developed an early consciousness of the beauty of this china and a love of it that has lasted the ensuing years of my life. When I was six years old, my mother discarded one of her broken dishes in the dustbin. Without her knowledge I slipped the pieces out and washed them. To my young eyes, they were much prettier than the pink and white china dishes I had received as a recent birthday present. Many happy hours of make-believe were spent playing with these "treasures" in my playhouse. Although it was not until years later I learned that this blue and white china was called Flow Blue, unknowingly, I had become a collector of it by the time I entered first grade.

My ancestors were English, so it is understandable that my mother would inherit a lovely old blue and white platter which had been brought to this country from England. It was one of her prized possessions, and I remember well that she kept it high on a shelf in a closed closet. On winter evenings she would take it down for me to admire. She did not permit me to hold it until I was grown. Until that time I was allowed to rub my hands over it while she carefully held it on her lap. I loved the beautiful scene of Windsor castle pictured in its center. Since I was the only daughter, my mother reminded me that someday it would be mine.

Years later, after my parents died, I was dismayed to discover that the platter was missing from their home. I would not be telling the truth if I did not say that my heart was broken. This family keepsake meant more to me than anything they could have left me. I only hope that whoever has it is as happy with it as I would have been.

The Flow Blue china you will see pictured in this book is from my collection and is the harvest of many collecting years. It has been an enjoyable, delightful experience acquiring each and every piece. Above all, my family has been very patient with me and my mania, and to them I give special thanks.

Early in my collecting I was told by dealers that Flow Blue was extremely scarce and difficult to collect. The challenge was impossible to resist. From then on, I visited antique shops across the country, taking in all the flea markets and antique shows that time would permit.

Discovering that auctions were a good source, I attended hundreds. If a Flow Blue piece were described as "mint," it was almost certain to fall in my hands. Sometimes I became so overjoyed with a successful acquisition that I really wasn't aware of how much I had bid for it. It wasn't long before people realized that I was an avid collector, and I acquired the nickname, the "Flow Blue Lady" in collecting circles.

Since Flow Blue is becoming more rare and expensive, it is becoming quite difficult to complete a dinner set made before 1870. Pieces are not impossible to find, but scarcity makes the search very competitive. If the item is in mint condition, a premium price will usually be demanded and paid.

Some collectors prefer to pick a pattern and collect only that pattern. I started that way, but it was not long before I found myself collecting a variety of patterns. At present, I am matching four complete dinner sets.

The Flow Blue featured in this book can be dated from a period starting in approximately 1835 and ending in the early 1900s. Some patterns are more scarce than others and, therefore, are more highly prized. Many of the pieces are not a deep blue, but this does not indicate that they are not Flow Blue. The cobalt used in producing that very deep blue was expensive, and substitute pigments were sometimes used. As a result, there may be some variation in the shades and tints of blue encountered. The blue glaze was induced to "flow" by the addition of lime or chloride of ammonia in the sagger during firing.

As you collect you will learn to discern the age of a piece by its weight and the visible wear on it. If it is not cracked or chipped, that fact will help you determine what to pay for it. The backstamp usually will give the name of the pattern and the maker, so you will soon learn how to identify the marks. This book contains photographs of the backstamps of most of the potters represented.

Where known, all of the pieces illustrated have been dated and their makers identified. Prices accompanying each item are provided to give a general concept of the present value range for that particular piece. However, it is important to remember that demand and quality also play a big part, and prices will vary in different regions of the country.

If I have made any mistakes in presenting the material in this book, they were not intentional. It is my sincere wish that this guide will add to your knowledge of Flow Blue china and aid you in your quest for it. Best of luck in your search.

The Flow Blue China of Staffordshire

In the limited space allotted to this introduction, it would be impossible to give a complete history of pottery making as it has evolved through the centuries. However, the following summary may help the reader or collector to place the development of Flow Blue china (particularly that from Staffordshire, England), in proper perspective.

It is fascinating to read that by the Tang Dynasty, 618-907 A.D., the Chinese had succeeded in producing a true porcelain. By the 18th century, when trade became legalized between China and Western Europe, Chinese pottery and porcelain production was already a highly evolved art form.

The Chinese were employing underglaze blue as early as the 9th century and, in 1351, began using cobalt blue which they called Mohammedan Blue, and which they obtained from the Mideast. By the 16th century, Chinese potters had devised a means of refining local cobalt, which undoubtedly made the production of pieces glazed in cobalt far less expensive. Other glazes and enamels of every hue had also been mastered by Chinese potters, and the beauty of their craftsmanship was highly esteemed by the privileged classes of the Continent and England.

An enormous export trade in Chinese porcelains sprang up in 1720 when Emperor K'ang Hsi granted licenses to certain Chinese merchants in Canton to engage in trade with the "foreign devils." Primarily these merchants dealt with the various East Indies Companies whose sailing ships returned to their Dutch and English home ports with holds bursting with products from the Chinese porcelain producing center of Ching-tè Chên located four hundred miles from Canton. During the reign of Emperor K'ang Hsi, in addition to the Imperial factory, 3,000 kilns were in fulltime operation in Ching-tè Chên.

In the early years of the 18th century, Chinese Export porcelain became so popular in England that the British East Indies Company stocked its offices with chests of sample dishes, making it possible for patrons to order custom-designed tea sets, dinner sets, and decorative pieces. In the latter half of the 18th century, more and more Chinese porcelain was specifically created in Western shapes and in made-to-order designs.

Chinese Blue and White and Nankin wares, in particular, found favor in the Western world then, and now are exhibited in museums as fine examples of the potter's art. It is understandable that English potters would make a concerted effort to reproduce these popular imports.

Although there were other areas in England producing ceramic wares at this time, it was the potters of the Staffordshire District who eventually succeeded in producing and marketing a product that became dominant both locally and abroad. Staffordshire was to become world-famous for the quantity and quality of its pottery and porcelain in the next 150 years.

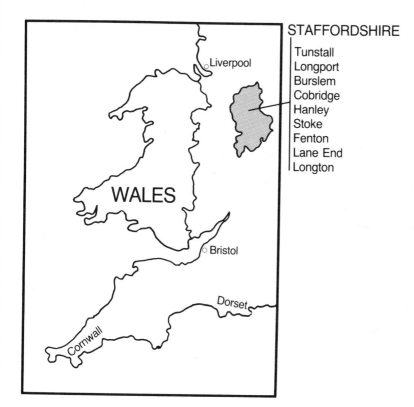

STAFFORDSHIRE

Tunstall
Longport
Burslem
Cobridge
Hanley
Stoke
Fenton
Lane End
Longton

From this small corner of England, measuring only nine miles long and three miles wide, came a majority of the Flow Blue china illustrated in this book.

The 18th century was a period of great technological growth in the Staffordshire potteries. The use of plaster of paris molds was introduced c. 1745. Application of transfer prints made from copper engravings followed in about 1755, and the stage was almost set for mass-producing and exporting dinnerware and other sets by the thousands. The final breakthrough occurred in 1765 when Josiah Wedgwood introduced Queen's Ware, a light but sturdy cream-colored earthenware body which Wedgwood is still producing today.

The earliest Staffordshire Flow Blue examples collectors will encounter may have been made on a stoneware body. These earlier patterns manifest a distinct Chinese influence in design motifs. As the Victorian era evolved (1837-1901), styles changed in dinnerware, and patterns became more baroque. Later pieces will be found to be on a fine, semiporcelain body closely related to Wedgwood's Queen's Ware.

Changes in contour will also be noted. Earlier Flow Blue plates frequently were twelve- or fourteen-paneled, with the panels possessing straight edges. The matching serving pieces from this period will be octagonal in shape, exhibiting angular rather than rounded contours.

The introduction of gold as a decorative enhancement on Flow Blue took place in the 1860s. Sugar bowls and creamers became smaller in size during these same years, as granulated sugar supplanted loaf sugar.

It has become common in the Flow Blue collecting field to divide the production periods into three phases: Early (c. 1835-1850), Middle (c. 1850-1870), and Late (c. 1880-1900). However, I have decided to present the patterns in this book by groups rather than by dates.

The categories are Oriental, Floral, Scenic, and Miscellaneous. Within these categories, each piece photographed is accompanied with pertinent facts to aid the collector, plus the approximate date of manufacture, and an *estimate* of the current value of the item. It is interesting to note that identical patterns were frequently produced by different potters. Several examples will be shown of these duplications.

Flow Blue was produced in other forms besides dinner sets at Staffordshire. If you are lucky you might encounter any of the following: tea services, cheese dishes, egg cups, jardinieres, pin trays, candlesticks, chamber pots, punch bowls and cups, chocolate pots, soup tureens with trays and ladles, compotes, toy dishes, vases, pitchers, and wash sets.

Other countries also manufactured Flow Blue from 1835 to 1900. The most noteworthy were Holland, Germany, and Portugal, but since most of the pieces from my collection originated in Staffordshire, England, the story of the Flow Blue produced in other countries must await the writing of another book.

Marks Section

In addition to noting the potter's backstamp, collectors should be alert for other marking clues that can help to identify and date the Flow Blue china produced in Staffordshire.

Diamond-shaped British Registry marks were impressed or printed on the bottoms of pieces produced between the years of 1842 and 1883.

British Registry Marks
Year and Month Letters

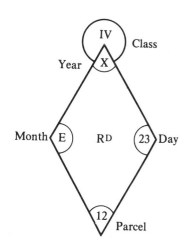

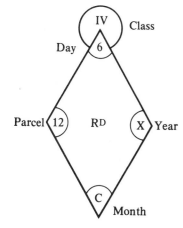

1842-67
Year Letter at Top

A	= 1845	N	= 1864
B	= 1858	O	= 1862
C	= 1844	P	= 1851
D	= 1852	Q	= 1866
E	= 1855	R	= 1861
F	= 1847	S	= 1849
G	= 1863	T	= 1867
H	= 1843	U	= 1848
I	= 1846	V	= 1850
J	= 1854	W	= 1865
K	= 1857	X	= 1842
L	= 1856	Y	= 1853
M	= 1859	Z	= 1860

1868-83
Year Letter at Right

A	= 1871	L	= 1882
C	= 1870	P	= 1877
D	= 1878	S	= 1875
E	= 1881	U	= 1874
F	= 1873	V	= 1876
H	= 1869	W	= Mar. 1-6 1878
I	= 1872		
J	= 1880	X	= 1868
K	= 1883	Y	= 1879

Months
(Both Periods)

A = December
B = October
C or O = January
D = September
E = May
G = February
H = April
I = July
K = November (and December 1860)
M = June
R = August (and September 1st-19 1857)
W = March

From 1884 on, the diamond shape was discontinued and Registry numbers, only, were employed. These numbers began with the number one in January, 1884, and proceeded to the number 331707 in January, 1899. Numbers higher than 360000 will indicate that a piece so marked was produced after 1900.

Flow Blue china marked with the words "Trade Mark" was produced after the Trade Mark Act of 1862. The word "Limited" or "Ltd" is found on pieces made after c. 1880. "Made in England" identifies pieces produced in the 20th century.

The following pages picture backstamps of Flow Blue pieces pictured in this book.

Johnson Bros., England

Wedgwood & Co., Ltd., England

Wood & Son, England

John Maddock & Sons, England

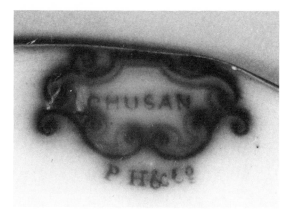

P H & Co., England

W. Adams & Co., England

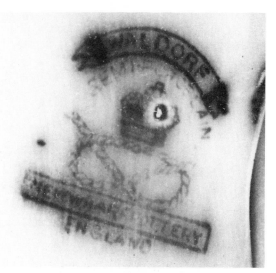

New Wharf Pottery (T. & R. Godwin), England

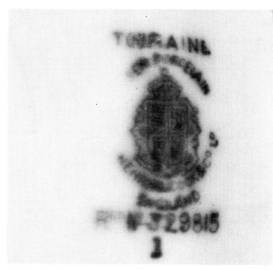

Henry Alcock & Co., Ltd., England

Ridgway, England

W. H. Grindley & Co., England

Davenport, England

Petrus Regout & Co., Maastricht, Holland

Alfred Meakin, Ltd., England

Edward Walley, England

Patterns by Categories

Oriental

Amoy

Twelve-sided, paneled plate, ironstone, 6½″ diameter, features floral reserves around a wide, dark blue band. Center depicts two mandarin figures—one seated, the other standing. There is a fringed parasol between them. Impressed anchor mark (Davenport). Made in England. C. 1844.

$30-45

Amoy

This semiporcelain bowl has a 2″ blue border. Diameter is 10½″. There are two ropes, one of white dainty flowers and the other of blue, garlanding the border. Around the well is a chain of small, lacy flowers. Center scene shows three mandarin figures. Two are seated and the third is standing and leaning on a long pole. This pattern is an interesting combination of Oriental and Victorian design. Marked Amoy, W. R. (Ridgway) England. C. 1845.

$50-65

Chapoo

Large, eight-sided sugar bowl, 9″ high, has a scene with a pagoda, an island linked by a small bridge, and a large flowering tree. Handles are open-ended. Marked J. Wedgwood, England. C. 1850.

$195-225

Chine

Scalloped chop plate with 13½″ diameter has center scene with a large chalet at the left. It is situated at the edge of a body of water. At center right is a boat. To the far right is a small building. In the background are mountains and a towered building. Well is wreathed in dahlialike flowers. The 2½″ border is cobalt with white embossing. Five reserves of a towered building with classical pillars decorate the border. Maker unknown. Marked England. C. 1880.

$65-75

Chusan

This 8″ ironstone plate has fourteen small panels with a wide, dark blue border containing scrolls and flowers. In the center of the deep well is a teahouse. To the right are two figures standing on a bridge; on the left is a large willow tree. Marked P. H. & Co., England. C. 1850.

$45-55

Fairy Villas (III)

Gently scalloped, semiporcelain 10″ bowl in dark blue cobalt glaze features embossed scrolls and bars and bouquets of flowers on the wide rim. Well of the bowl is outlined with a floral chain. In the center is a teahouse located on the shore of a body of water on which a boat with two figures sails. To the left and the center are trees and a pagoda. Marked W. Adams & Co., England. C. 1891.

$50-60

Hong Kong

This 7½″ ironstone plate is twelve-sided. Rim is outlined in dark blue, and groupings of leaves and chrysanthemums circle the border. The deep well is outlined with a diaper design in deep cobalt blue. Center scene features small islands with houses at the top and one large island with a house at the bottom. Six little birds fly in upper center. Made by Charles Meigh. Marked Improved Stone China, England. C. 1845.

$45-50

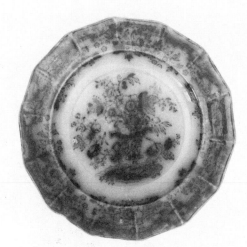

Indian Stone

The 7″ ironstone plate shown is fourteen-sided and paneled with a 1″ border composed of large and small flowers combined with very dark leaves. Center design has a handled urn filled with a mixed bouquet. Made by Edward Walley. Marked E W with urn and scroll, England. C. 1850.

$40-50

Japanese

The borders of this 6″ saucer and 2½″ cup are decorated with alternating cartouche and diaper designs. In the center and on the right is a small footed table upon which an urn with a bouquet of flowers is displayed. To the center left is a small tree with flowers circled on the top. Made by Wood & Baggaley. Marked W & B. England. C. 1875

Set: $45-55

Kyber

In this set of dishes the 10″ plates are paneled and twelve-sided. A scene featuring a teahouse, tree, and fence is repeated in five reserves on the border. In the center a pagoda, tall tree, and large urn with flowers are pictured in a stylized Japanese landscape. Marked W. Adams & Co., England. C. 1891.

$55-75

Manilla

Handleless, 3½″ stoneware cup shows a scene of a teahouse and a pavilion, each on separate islands. Joining the islands is a bridge upon which a guide with a lantern lights a traveler's way. Made by Podmore Walker. Impressed P.W. & Co., England. C. 1845.

$55-65

Oriental

This 5″ stoneware creamer has a dark blue transfer design around the lip. On both sides is depicted a body of water with a large temple to the right. A sailboat is shown in the center and in the background are other buildings. In the left foreground is a kneeling man holding a spear. Made by William Ridgway. Marked W.R., England. C. 1891.

$60-75

Oriental

On the wide border of this 10″ plate are medallions of a temple which alternate with floral patterns. The center scene shows a temple to the right, and at the left is a man on a camel. There are two figures standing nearby. Around the well is a wreathlike design. Marked Petrus Regout & Co., Maastricht. Made in Holland. C. 1900.

$40-45

Tonquin

Ironstone cup is twelve-sided and is 3¾″ tall. On the inside is a band of circle designs with peonies alternating with loop-like figures. On the exterior a tall tree is to the right, and, in the distance, is an island with buildings. Two men in a boat occupy the foreground. Made by Joseph Heath, England. C. 1845.

$60-65

Willow

Small, 7″ platter has the typical willow design in deep cobalt blue. Made by Ridgway & Co., England. C. 1880.

$25-35

Floral

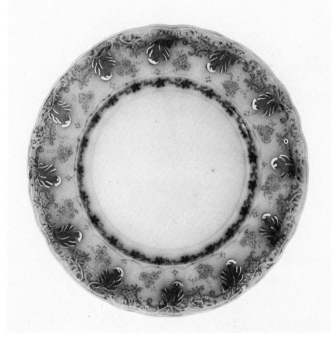

Astoria

The rim of this scalloped, semiporcelain 10″ plate is outlined in gold around the edge and embossed with white beading. Marked Johnson Bros., England. C. 1900

$30-36

Astoria

Matching, round fruit bowl with handles has 9″ diameter. Marked Johnson Bros., England. C. 1900

$50-65

Astoria

Gravy boat, 7″ from handle to lip. Marked Johnson Bros., England. C. 1900.

$35-45

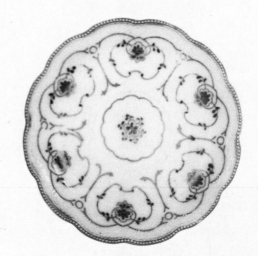

Beaufort

Scalloped, 6″ saucer has beaded and embossed rim and delicate, stylized floral and leaf reserves. Marked W. H. Grindley, England. C. 1903.

$15-20

Belmont

Small, 8″ tureen is complete with 9″ underplate and 12″ ladle. The lid and the underplate are scalloped. Groups of rose-like flowers and sprigs surround all three pieces. The edges are gilded. Made by J.H.W. & Sons. Marked Hanley, England. C. 1905.

$150-170

Begonia

This 12″ tureen is beautiful with its 14″ underplate and 12″ ladle in semiporcelain. Begonia-and-leaf design is enhanced with white embossing and gold edges. Marked Johnson Bros., England. C. 1880.

$175-225

Birds

On the border of this plate are six floral reserves separated by a diaper design. The outer edge is indented at each medallion. Center scene depicts two phoenixes with long trailing tail feathers perched on a tree limb. The name of the pattern is blurred, so this name has been given to catalog it. Maker unknown. Marked England. C. 1900.

$30-35

Blue Rose

Small, semiporcelain 6″ plate has a scalloped edge that is beaded and embossed with small flowers. It has a wide, deep cobalt blue border and gold highlights. The pattern is similar to the Iowa pattern. Marked W. H. Grindley, England. C. 1900.

$20-25

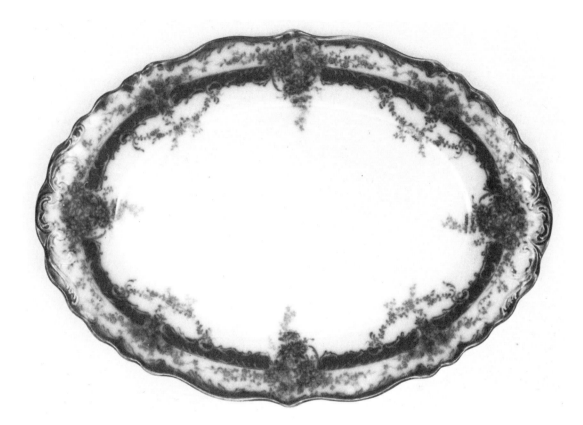

Bouquet

Semiporcelain, 15″ platter has scalloped edges outlined with a dark blue band and white embossing. There are four large groups of daisylike flowers joined with a wide band of dark blue and outlined with gold. These floral reserves alternate with sprigs that enter the well of the platter. Marked Henry Alcock, England. C. 1895.

$60-75

Cambridge

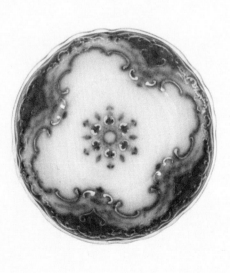

This 5″ saucedish is from one of my lovely sets of dishes. It has a scalloped contour with a rim edged in gold. Reserves of scrolled embossing accented in gold frame the well. In the center is a six-pointed snowflake. Marked Alfred Meakin, England. C. 1891.

$10-12

Canister

This 6″ coffee canister is decorated with small flowers, leaves, and sprigs in deep cobalt blue. Lid is missing. Maker unknown. Unmarked, but matches similar pieces marked Germany. C. 1890.

$30-40

Cheese Dish

There is no name for this pattern so I have listed it as above in order to catalog it. It measures 9″ x 7″ x 4½″. The bottom has a large band of dark blue with a rose in the center. The lid is also outlined with the same dark band. The design on the lid is of roses and leaves. The handle is dark blue. Maker unknown. Marked Staffordshire, England. C. 1880.

$150-185

Clarence

Scalloped rim of this 10″ semiporcelain plate has a white beading over cobalt blue. The 2″ border design consists of cartouches alternating with floral reserves whose tendrils extend into the well. Lacy white embossing outlines the center. Marked W. H. Grindley, England. C. 1880.

$30-35

8″ PLATE - JP

Clayton

Scalloped, 9″ semiporcelain plate has a ¼″ edging of embossed flowers. White daisies decorate the cobalt border. Dainty blue flowers extend into the well. The same design is depicted on the matching cup. Marked Johnson Bros., England. C. 1900.

$30-35

Clayton

Semiporcelain cup with 2½″ diameter has shaping and embossing at base which echoes contour of matching plate.

Clayton

Saucer has a 6″ diameter and is back-marked the same as the plate. Price is for the cup and saucer set.

$40-50

Dresden

Semiporcelain 10″ plate has a border of blue onion forms and small sprigs. A ring of leaves encircles the well. In the center is a stylized floral and leaf arrangement. This is similar to the Onion pattern made by Altertons. Maker unknown. Marked Dresden, England. C. 1891.

$28-33

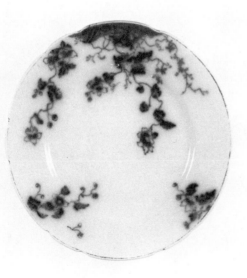

Duchess

Slightly scalloped, 7″ semiporcelain plate has a simple, assymetrical floral motif. Marked W. H. Grindley, England. C. 1890.

$15-18

Flora

The collar of this 12″ semiporcelain wash pitcher is scalloped, and the bulbous body is molded in wavy swirls. A floral pattern with gold lustre graces the collar and sides. Maker unknown. Marked Flora, England. C. 1880.

Companion washbasin, 17″ in diameter, is decorated with matching swirls and floral motif touched with gold lustre. Also marked Flora, England. Price given is for the two-piece set.

$375-400

Flora

Toothbrush holder in this set is 5½″ high. Marked Flora, England. C. 1880.

$40-45

Flora

Round, three-piece soap dish measures 5″ in diameter and is complete with soap drainer. Marked Flora, England. C. 1880.

$65-75$

Florida

Semiporcelain, 9″ plate has a six-sided, scalloped contour. The ornate border is complemented by white well circled with a lacy fleur-de-lis design. Marked Johnson Bros., England. C. 1905.

$35-40$

Iowa

Scalloped, 6″ semiporcelain plate has beaded edge. Center design of full-blown rose, leaves, and small blossoms is in underglaze cobalt blue accented with embossing and gold. This pattern is identical to Blue Rose by Grindley. Made by Arthur Wilkinson. Marked Royal Staffordshire Pottery, England. C. 1905.

$15-23

Iris

Beautiful, skirted pitcher has a scalloped gold lip and measures 8″ high. Design of dark blue irises and leaves is heavily outlined in gold. Embossing on top, center, and bottom, is lightly accented. Maker unknown. Marked England. C. 1900.

$100-125

Ivy

The pattern name is not stamped on the bottom of this 7½″ pitcher, but an identical one has been seen which was marked with this pattern name. An embossed geometric design circles the base. Maker unknown. Marked England. C. 1900.

$80-95

La Belle

Feathery scrolls outlined in gold decorate the scalloped ends of this 13½″ celery dish. Cobalt, fading to white, glazes the outer edges. Floral sprays in deep cobalt are scattered informally. On the underside of the dish are sprigs of flowers, and the base is encircled with a gold band. Made by Wheeling Pottery, Wheeling, West Virginia. Marked La Belle China. C. 1900.

$100-125

La Belle

Charming 5″ syrup pitcher has a pewter collar and lid. Also marked La Belle China. C. 1900.

$55-65

Lugano

The scalloped rim of semiporcelain 9″ plate is embossed and outlined in gold. Five groups of small peachlike blossoms are on the 2″ blue border. Sprigs and blossoms extend into the well. Some of the flowers and foliage are touched with gold. Marked Ridgway, England. C. 1910.

$35-40

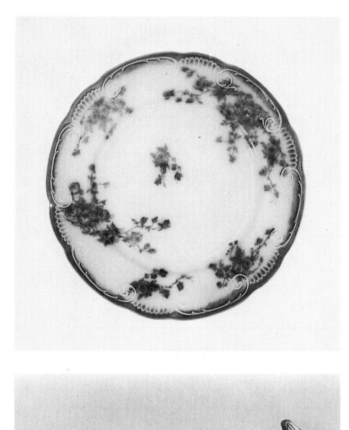

Marechal Niel

Unevenly scalloped 9″ semiporcelain underplate has feathery embossing alternating with half-circles. There are sprays of small roses and buds. One spray is placed off center. Marked W. H. Grindley, England. C. 1895.

$40-50

Marechal Niel

Gravy boat in this pattern measures 7″ from handle to lip. Marked W. H. Grindley, England. C. 1895.

$55-65

Marechal Niel

Matching 3″ butter pat is also marked W.
H. Grindley, England. C. 1895.

$10-15

Saucer - JP

Marguerite

Scalloped 9″ semiporcelain plate is edged
in gold. Six reserves of marguerites are
grouped around the border, with sprigs
from each spray extending into the well.
Marked W. H. Grindley, England. C.
1891.

$40-50

Melbourne

The 14″ platter has a gently scalloped rim that is outlined in gold with white beading. Around the wide border are floral reserves on a diaper design. Marked W. H. Grindley, England. C. 1900.

$60-75

Melbourne

Matching 9″ plate is also marked W. H. Grindley, England. C. 1900.

$30-40

Oakland

Sides of 3″ square, semiporcelain butter pat are gently curved, and the edges are touched with gold. Dogwood blossoms and large leaves cover the entire dish. Marked John Maddock & Sons, England. C. 1898.

$10-13

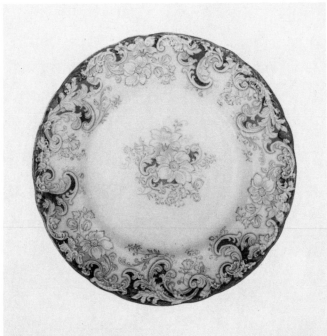

Ormonde

The slightly scalloped border of this 9″ semiporcelain plate is printed in light and dark blue. The border motif consists of scrolls, flowers, and foliage, and is repeated in the center of the plate. Marked Alfred Meakin England. C. 1891.

$30-35

Osborne

Dark blue chrysanthemums and leaves decorate the upper half of 7″ semiporcelain pitcher. Lower half of pitcher has embossed leaves which are outlined in gold. Marked Ridgway, England. C. 1900.

$45-50$

Pansy

Gently scalloped, semiporcelain rectangular platter measures 13″ x 15″. Scrolled reserves of pansies and leaves form the border design. Edges are touched with gold. Marked Johnson Bros., England. C. 1880.

$150-175$

Pansy

The 1″ band at the top of this 7½″ semi-porcelain pitcher is in dark cobalt blue with diagonal gold highlights. Bottom rim is also dark blue. Pansies and foliage appear in the middle with sprigs flowering to the bottom. Maker unknown, but probably J. B. Marked England. C. 1880

$70-85

Pansy

Semiporcelain 13″ vase is from a pair that has been in my collection for several years, and they are lovely. Pansies in light and dark blue outlined in gold cover one side of each vase. Handles, rims, and band are richly decorated in gold. Maker unknown. Marked England. C. 1900.

Each: $135-150

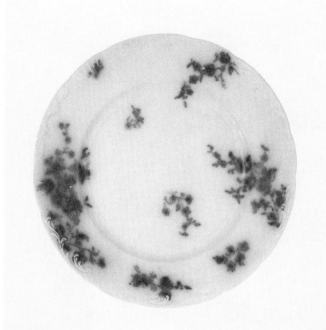

Rose

Contour of 9″ semiporcelain plate is gently scalloped and gilt edged. Scrolls and
feathery designs are embossed around
the rim. Casual groupings of wild roses
and foliage trim the border and well.
Marked W. H. Grindley, England. C.
1893.

$25-30

Cup & Saucer

St. Louis

Scalloped border of 9″ semiporcelain
plate is accentuated with beading and
embossing which follow the contour.
Three bunches of small flowers overlap
the dark blue border, with sprays extending into the well. Marked Johnson Bros.,
England. C. 1900.

$30-35

Sheraton

Small, oval, 9″ semiporcelain underplate belongs to a tureen. Edge is banded in dark blue with a narrow floral border. Inside the border, floral swags circle the well. Maker unknown. Marked England. C. 1900.

$25-30

Touraine

This scalloped, 9″ semiporcelain plate has a wide, dark blue border trimmed in gold. Five floral sprays adorn the border and well. Marked Henry Alcock, England. C. 1898.

$30-35

Touraine

Cup measures 2½″. Saucer has a 6″ diameter. Marked Henry Alcock, England. C. 1900. Price is for the set.

$45-55

Touraine

Covered vegetable bowl in this pattern has a 9″ diameter. Marked Henry Alcock, England. C. 1900.

$135-150

Touraine

This 9″ semiporcelain plate is identical to the pattern by Alcock. The blue may be a different shade. It is possible that Alcock made the pattern first. Marked Stanley Pottery, England. C. 1898.

$30-35

Verona

Bulbous 7″ semiporcelain pitcher shown has a blue collar that is outlined with gold and beading in relief. From top downward is a wash of lighter blue upon which are placed one large and two small roselike flowers from which swags of daisies extend. The base is circled in light and deeper blue. White beading and small scrolls are outlined in gold. Marked Ridgway, England. C. 1910.

$110-135

Virginia

Scalloped contour of 6″ semiporcelain saucer is embossed and touched with gold. This pattern has a grapelike vine with three groups of large leaves which are outlined in gold. Marked John Maddock & Son, England. C. 1891.

$18-25

Saucer- JP

Waldorf

This 10″ semiporcelain platter has a dark cobalt blue scalloped edge. Bouquets of flowers decorate the edge with sprigs extending into the well. A dark blue bouquet is in the center. Marked New Wharf Pottery, England. C. 1892.

$75-85

Warwick

Semiporcelain 5″ syrup pitcher has a pewter top and collar. Below the collar is embossing, and gold lustre has been applied over it. The bowl is covered with wild roses and leaves. This is an American-made piece. Marked Warwick China Co. C. 1900.

$40-50

Warwick Pansy

Small semiporcelain 5″ relish dish has an allover pattern of pansies and small blossoms. Gold lustre has been applied to the scalloped, embossed edge. This was also made in America. Marked Warwick China Co. C. 1900.

$30-35

Addendum to Bibliography

Williams, Petra. *Flow Blue China An Aid to Identification*. Jeffersontown, Kentucky: Fountain House East, 1971

———. *Flow Blue China II*. Jeffersontown, Kentucky: Fountain House East, 1973.

———. *Flow Blue China and Mulberry Ware*. Jeffersontown, Kentucky: Fountain House East, 1975.

Scenic

Coburg

Twelve-sided 9″ ironstone plate has panels decorated with grapelike leaves. Center scene shows a tall tree at right center and a temple in the distance. To the left is a large temple. In the foregound are three persons; one is standing with a large pole across his back. Made by John Edwards. Marked J. E., England. C. 1860.

$50-75

Cows

Although there is no pattern name for this 15½″ x 17″ semiporcelain platter, it has been called "Cows" or "Cow Plate" for as long as I can remember. The transfer design is in a dark slate blue without much flowing; however, the glaze is heavily flowed on the underside. The wide rim contains cartouches alternating with reserves of the cow scene. Marked Wedgwood & Co., Ltd., England. C. 1900.

$225-250

Cows

Semiporcelain 10″ plate features cows on a plain with hillside in the background. Plate is bordered with three different views. Marked Wedgwood & Co., Ltd., England. C. 1900.

$45-50

English Scene

Dark blue border of this semiporcelain 8½″ bowl is glazed with various sized flowers. A lacy chain encircles the well. In the center is a stone building with a round tower. A small body of water and a flower-strewn bank occupy the foreground. Tall trees frame the scene. Maker unknown, but probably of English manufacture. C. 1880.

$60-70

English Scene

Semiporcelain 8″ pitcher does not have a pattern name, so to catalog it I have called it "English Scene." The lip is glazed with a wide blue band and white leaves. Both sides of this eight-paneled pitcher are decorated with the same scene. The footed base has a design around it that matches the lip. Maker unknown. Marked England. C. 1850.

$65-70

English Scenery

Peonies on a blue background form the border of this semiporcelain 7″ bone dish. The center scene shows a path edged with low trees leading to a castle. On the hillside to the left are two rows of trees, and at the bottom is an old fence. Three people are strolling on the path to the castle. Marked Wood & Sons, England. C. 1880.

$30-35

Jenny Lind

Small, 3½" semiporcelain pitcher features an overall scene. Pattern honored coloratura soprano Jenny Lind (also known as the Swedish Nightingale). Maker unknown. Marked England. C. 1896.

$50-60

Lincoln's Home

This 9½" souvenir plate shows Abraham Lincoln's house in Springfield, Illinois. The oval insert bears his portrait. On the border are eight reserves of dahlias and forget-me-nots framed on a blue background. The overall design matches the Washington's Home souvenir plate which also appears in this book. Marked Petrus Regout, Maastricht, Holland. C. 1909.

$45-55

Turkey

Slightly scalloped shape of 10″ game plate is enhanced by a deep blue, embossed border with contour outlined in gold. Wild turkeys in center motif are executed in shades of blue. Marked Doulton, England. C. 1900.

$75-100

Washington's Home

A 9½″ souvenir plate shows Washington's home at Mount Vernon and an insert with his portrait. Border has eight framed floral reserves on a blue background. Design matches border of Lincoln's Home souvenir plate, but features different flowers. From the Presidents Souvenir Series of plates. Marked Petrus Regout, Made in Holland. C. 1909.

$45-55

Woodland

Scalloped, 9½″ soup bowl has a flat rim decorated with sprays of prunus blossoms. A transfer design scene has been applied to the well, around which flying birds circle. Larger birds feeding on the ground occupy the foreground creating a three-dimensional effect. Marked Brown Field & Son, England. C. 1880.

$45-60

Woodland

Scene on slant-sided, 2½″ cup from this set is a bordered transfer print of a horse-drawn load of hay. Prunus blossoms echo motif on rim of bowl. Marked Brown Field & Son, England. C. 1880.

$25-30

Miscellaneous

Argyle

Six-sided, 6″ sugar bowl is topped with a plumed finial. Gold touched plumes and flowers decorate the lid and bowl. Embossed design on footed base is also brushed with gold. Marked W. H. Grindley, England. C. 1896.

$50-60

Argyle

Blue plumes and floral sprays decorate the border of the twelve-sided, 6″ Argyle saucer. Embossed scrolls are accented in gold. Marked W. H. Grindley, England. C. 1896.

$20-25

Blossoms

Dainty, 2¼″ demitasse cup could possibly be a child's cup. It has a band that is paneled with little flowers on alternating light and darker blue backgrounds. Small sprays of prunus blossoms decorate the sides. Marked Ridgway, England. C. 1845.

$20-25

Colonial

Semiporcelain 14″ platter has a scalloped contour. Stylized floral and leaf design is symmetrically arranged in an overall design. Embossed scrolls are touched with gold. Marked J. & G. Meakin, England. C. 1891.

$75-100

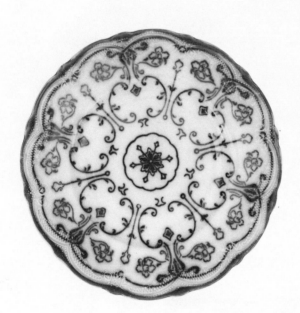

Saucer - IP

Conway

Outer edge of 9″ scalloped plate is glazed in dark blue. Delicate design of beading and scrolls is embossed and wiped to contrast with lighter blue ground. Six reserves ring the snowflake-like center medallion. Marked New Wharf Pottery, England. C. 1891.

$40-45

Delamere

Scalloped semiporcelain 6″ plate features flowing forms in dark blue which are highlighted with gold. Marked Henry Alcock, England. C. 1900.

$20-25

Diamond

Dark blue-and-white 2¼″ cup is banded inside and out with diaper designs combined with a leaf motif. Pattern name is derived from diamond-shaped medallions. Maker unknown. Marked England. C. 1900.

$20-25

Feather Edge

Creamy-white, eight-sided 12½″ platter is an early stoneware piece. Embossed edge is glazed in a feathery brushstroke of cobalt blue. I do not consider this as Flow Blue, but some collectors and dealers classify it as such. Marked Clementson & Young, England. C. 1845.

$55-60

Fish Plate

This 8″ semiporcelain plate shows a scalloped contour with dark cobalt and gilt trim. Within the dark blue edges are gold medallions. Two fish swim in the water among the weeds. Maker unknown. Unmarked, but probably of English origin. C. 1910.

$35-40

Fruit

Semiporcelain 8″ plates are from a series of fruit plates. The rims and bands around the wells are gilded. An embossed basketweave pattern decorates the 1″ borders. In the center of each is a grouping of fruits and leaves glazed in deep cobalt. I consider these pieces borderline Flow Blue. Marked P. Regout & Co., Holland. C. 1900.

$25-30

Game Birds

Graceful scene depicted on semiporcelain 11″ vase is glazed in varying shades and tints of blue. It shows a female bird on the nest, with the male bird perched on a limb nearby. Maker unknown. Marked England. C. 1900.

$140-165

Gravy Boat

Unnamed, semiporcelain gravy boat measures 7″ from handle to lip. I have cataloged it as above until I discover the pattern name for it. Two lines circle the rim interior and continue down the handle. All designs are glazed in a deep cobalt blue. Maker unknown. Unmarked, probably English. C. 1900.

$25-30

Imperial

Covered semiporcelain 11″ vegetable dish has four main scalloped sides. The lid and the foot follow the same contour. Small flowers and elaborate scrolls circle the bowl. The ornate lid is crowned with an embossed escutcheon and deep blue floral finial. Marked Myatt, Son & Co., England. C. 1891.

$85-125

Jardiniere

Semiporcelain, 8″ jardiniere has blurred floral motif in cobalt. The pattern is unknown so I have simply cataloged it as above. Collar is scalloped, and white embossed swirls and a featherlike design cover the body of this four-footed piece. Marked Bridgewood & Sons, England. C. 1900.

$100-125

Jewel

Semiporcelain, 3″ butter pat.

$15-20

Jewel

Semiporcelain, 12″ platter has large scalloped edges that are embossed and outlined in deep cobalt and gold and five
reserves of lilylike designs that are executed in bold curves. Marked Johnson
Bros., England. C. 1900.

$60-75

Jewel

Also in the Jewel pattern is this 2½" demitasse cup with matching 4½" saucer. Marked Johnson Bros., England. Price is for the set.

$45-50

Knox

This 10″ semiporcelain platter has an unevenly scalloped edge with beaded embossing. Seven reserves with looped pen-
dants form an arched design. The center
medallion resembles a snowflake.
Marked New Wharf Pottery, England. C.
1890.

$60-75

Ladle

A dark blue floral design is applied to the
bowl and handle of this 7″ semiporcelain
ladle. Name of pattern and maker are unknown. Probably of English manufacture. C. 1880.

$40-50

Flora washbasin and pitcher—$375-400.

(l to r) Butter pats—$10-15, each. Demitasse cup and saucer set—$45-50. Large plate—$35-40. Soup bowl—$25-30. All in Jewel pattern.

Unnamed jardiniere—$100-125.

(l to r) La Belle syrup pitcher—$55-65.
La Belle relish dish—$100-125. Iris
pitcher—$100-125.

(l to r) Amoy plate—$30-45. Chusan plate—$45-55. Tonquin cup—$60-65.

Unnamed punch bowl—$275-300.

(l to r) Spinach cup and saucer—$35-40. Unnamed cheese dish—$150-185. Ivy pitcher—$80-95.

(l to r) Unnamed gravy boat—$25-30. Unnamed ladle—$40-50. Waldorf platter—$75-85. Pansy pitcher—$70-85.

(l to r) Oxford soup bowl—$25-30. Melbourne platter—$60-75. Astoria gravy boat—$35-45.

Chapoo sugar bowl—$195-225.

Jewel demitasse cups and saucers—$45-50 each set.

(l to r) Argyle sugar bowl—$50-65. Florida plate—$35-40. Verona pitcher—$110-135.

Cows platter—$225-250.

(l to r) Indian Stone plate—$40-50. Kyber plate—$55-75. Coburg plate—$50-75.

Pansy platter—$150-175.

(l to r) St. Louis plate—$30-35. Astoria fruit bowl—$50-65. Astoria plate—$30-35.

Turkey plate—$75-100.

(l to r) Cambridge saucedish—$10-12. Knox platter—$60-75. Clayton cup and saucer—$40-50.

La Francais

This semiporcelain 14″ platter has a scalloped, gilded edge. Embossed scrolls and fleurs-de-lis in gold lustre are printed over the wide, dark cobalt band. Marked French China Co. (This company was located in Sebring, Ohio.) C. 1900.

$40-50

Lorne   *8″ Soup*

Semiporcelain, 10″ plate has a scalloped, beaded edge outlined in cobalt blue. Six reserves with three-leaf clovers are placed around the border. Central medallion echoes border design. Marked W. H. Grindley, England. C. 1900.

$30-35

Lorne

Matching 2½" cup shows white embossing which also circles outer rim of plate. Marked W. H. Grindley, England. C. 1900.

Normandy

This semiporcelain 12½" platter has a lovely, deep scalloped edge, blue band, and ruffled embossing. Each scallop is outlined with a garland of small blossoms. Around the border are alternating large and small leaves in dark cobalt blue. The well is circled with a broken floral garland. Marked Johnson Bros., England. C. 1900.

$60-75

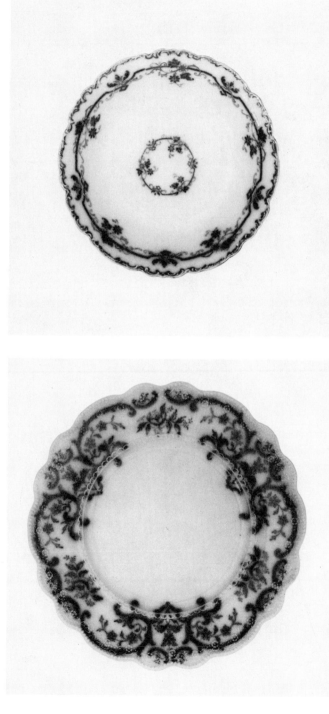

Oxford

Semiporcelain 7½″ soup bowl has deeply scalloped and embossed edges outlined in blue highlighted with gold. Light and deep blue floral reserves, joined by a deep blue line, circle the rim and extend into the bowl. Center design repeats border motif. Marked Johnson Bros., England. C. 1900.

$25-30

Portman

Embossed filigree and beading follow the contour of semiporcelain, scalloped 10″ plate. The outside rim has scrolls of heavy dark blue containing clusters of small flowers. Well is encircled with dainty embossing. Marked W. H. Grindley, England. C. 1890.

$30-35

Punch Bowl

Punch bowl, 8″ high with 15″ diameter, features allover design of flowers and leaves inside and out. Rim and pedestal are banded in a cobalt and light blue floral diaper. The pattern name is unknown. Marked Ridgway, England. C. 1845.

$275-300

Spinach

The 6″ semiporcelain saucer is decorated in boldly brushed, deep cobalt leaves. A thin cobalt band accents the rim. This pattern has been known as "Oatmeal" and "Turkey Feather." Marked Libertas. Made in Prussia. C. 1900.

Spinach

Matching cup measures 2½″ high and is circled with a cobalt band and spinach leaves.

Set: $45-55

Tile

A lone figure mans the tiller of a sailboat on a rolling sea, and corner medallions frame the scene on this 6″ x 6″ porcelain tile. Brush-applied cobalt glaze varies from very light to very deep blue. Unmarked. C. 1880.

$25-30

Trent

Gently scalloped 8″ semiporcelain plate
has a very wide dark cobalt border. The
glaze flows heavily on the underneath
side. Rim, inner edge of border, and border garlands are in gold. Fruits and foliage form the center design. Marked E.
Wood & Son, England. C. 1890.

$50-60

Tulip and Sprig

This twelve-sided 7″ stoneware plate has
a dark blue border. Four stylized tulips
alternating with four sprigs comprise the
main design. A small sprig is placed in
the center. This is a heavy stoneware
plate, and it shows a lot of wear. Marked
T Walker (impressed), England. C. 1845.

$40-50

Washbasin

Large semiporcelain washbasin measures
6″ x 15″ and has the same pattern as the
punch bowl, only the design is glazed in a
lighter blue. Marked Ridgway, England.
C. 1845.

$100-125

General Price Guide

Beginning collectors may find this general price guide to other pieces in Flow Blue helpful when determining if a piece of Flow Blue is offered at a fair price. Remember that values can vary by regions of the country and that the law of supply and demand applies to any form of collecting—Flow Blue included. Prices are for pieces in good-to-better condition.

Butter dish	$195+
Coffee server	300+
Teapot with lid	275+
Foot bath	575+
Washbasin	200+
Water pitcher for water bowl	275+
Chamber pot with lid	195+
Waste jar with lid	275+
Game plates	50+
Calendar plates	45+
Souvenir plates	50+
Fish plates	50+
Portrait plates	65+
Hatpin holders	50+
Hairpin tray	60+
Hair receiver	75+
Powder box	80+
Clock	250+
Umbrella stand	275+

Other Popular Patterns and Prices

Collectors will encounter other Flow Blue patterns as they seek to enlarge their collections. I have listed a few of these patterns and guide prices for the most commonly sought pieces. Bear in mind that prices are given for pieces in good-to-better condition and that regional differences will have an influence upon current selling prices.

Pattern	Plate	Cup/Saucer	Creamer/Sugar
Alaska	$35-50	$55+	$185+
Albany	35-40	45+	185+
Alberta	30-35	40+	165+
Amour	55-75	75+	300+
Beatrice	30-35	40+	165+
Brunswick	30-35	40+	165+
Canton	55-75	75+	300+
Cecil	30-35	45+	165+
Claremont	30-35	45+	165+
Clarissa	30-35	45+	165+
Dahlia	50-70	55+	190+
Eclipse	35-45	45+	180+
Floral	35-50	35+	175+
Florence	30-35	45+	165+
Formosa	65-80	75+	350+
Garland	35-40	45+	180+
Georgia	25-35	40+	175+
Jeddo	50-60	65+	250+
Linda	40-50	55+	185+
Lonsdale	35-50	45+	175+
Manhattan	30-40	40+	185+
Oregon	65-75	75+	325+
Rhone	65-75	75+	350+
Stanley	40-50	60+	225+
Temple	65-75	75+	325+
Watteau	70-80	85+	375+
Waverly	30-40	65+	200+

Bibliography

Blake, Sylvia Dugger. *Flow Blue.* Des Moines, Iowa: Wallace-Homestead Book Co., 1971.

Eberlein, Howard., and Ramsdell, Roger W. *The Practical Book of Chinaware,* rev. ed. Philadelphia and New York: J. B. Lippincott Co., 1925, 1948.

Fisher, Stanley W. *British Pottery and Porcelain.* New York: Bell Publishing Co., 1962.

Encyclopedia of Collectibles. Chicago, Illinois: Time-Life Books, 1980.

Williams, Petra. *Flow Blue China,* rev. ed. Jeffersontown, Kentucky: Fountain House East, 1981.

———*Flow Blue China II,* rev. ed. Jeffersontown, Kentucky: Fountain House East, 1981.

Index of Patterns

About the Author

Veneita Mason is well known as an authority on Flow Blue. Years of research and love for this china have culminated in the writing of this book. Her interests have been wide, as you can note from her professional background which includes history teacher, artist, realtor, interior designer, collector, floral designer, lecturer, and now, author. She likes to admit that she is also a wife, mother, and grandmother.

Author's collection.

Author's collection.

Author's collection.